The Moon and You

SATURN 5 MOON ROCKET
MOVING TO LAUNCH PAD 39A,
CAPE CANAVERAL, FLORIDA,
JULY 11, 1969

BABYLONIAN sin   BANGLA chad চাঁদ   CAMBODIAN khae   CANTONESE yút   CHOCTAW hashi

CHUMASH 'alahtin   DUTCH maan   ENGLISH moon   ESKIMO takret   FIJI vula   FRENCH lune

ARMENIAN khaldi Խալդի   ARABIC qamar قمر   APACHE tl'é'gona'áí   ALEUT tugidaq   AFRIKAANS maan

GAELIC gealach   GERMAN mond   GREEK mene μούν   HAITIAN CREOLE lalin   HAWAIIAN mahina

LAO pa:cha:n ພຣະຈັນ   LATIN luna   LITHUANIAN mẽnuo   MANDARIN CHINESE yuèliang 月亮   MAORI marama

KOREAN dal 달

JAPANESE tskuki 月

ITALIAN luna

INDONESIAN bulan

HINDI chandra चन्द्र

HEBREW ירח

10 · 9 · 8 · 7 · 6 · 5 · 4 · 3 · 2 · 1 LIFT-OFF!

NAHUATL meztli   NAVAJO tt'éhonaa'éí   NORSE mani   PAPAGO—PIMA mashad   POLISH ksiezye   PERSIAN mahi ماه دنیا

The Moon and You

Written by E.C. KRUPP
Illustrated by ROBIN RECTOR KRUPP

MACMILLAN PUBLISHING COMPANY
NEW YORK
MAXWELL MACMILLAN CANADA
TORONTO
MAXWELL MACMILLAN INTERNATIONAL
NEW YORK   OXFORD   SINGAPORE   SYDNEY

RUSSIAN луна

SANSKRIT mas

чч:

SKIDI PAWNEE pah

SPANISH luna

SWAHILI mwezi

SATURN 5
MOON ROCKET
LEAVES EARTH,
JULY 16, 1969.

SWEDISH måne   TURKISH ay   VIETNAMESE mặt trăng

For Edwin F. Krupp
(1921-1992),
systems engineer,
whose work
at Pad 39A
helped send
the first men
to the moon

Macmillan Publishing Company is part of the Maxwell Com-
munication Group of Companies.
Macmillan Publishing Company
866 Third Avenue
New York, NY 10022
Maxwell Macmillan Canada, Inc.
1200 Eglinton Avenue East
Suite 200
Don Mills, Ontario M3C 3N1
First edition
Printed in the United States of America

10 9 8 7 6 5 4 3 2 1

The text of this book is set in 14 pt. Century Schoolbook.
The illustrations are rendered in pencil on plate finish Strathmore.

Library of Congress Cataloging-in-Publication Data
Krupp, E. C. (Edwin C.), date.
The moon and you / written by E.C. Krupp ; illustrated by Robin
Rector Krupp. — 1st ed.
    p.   cm.
Summary: Provides information about Earth's nearest neighbor
in space, the moon, describing its phases, rotation, effect on our
tides, and some of the myths and legends about the Earth's
nearest neighbor in space.
ISBN 0-02-751142-1
1. Moon—Juvenile literature. [1. Moon.] I. Krupp, Robin
Rector, ill. II. Title.
QB582.K78 1993   523.3—dc20   92-16231

Thanks to Annie Bedian, Bian Depei, Lick Observatory, Thomas
E. Mails, Mount Wilson Observatory, National Aeronautics and
Space Administration (NASA), Palomar Observatory, and Space
Camp.

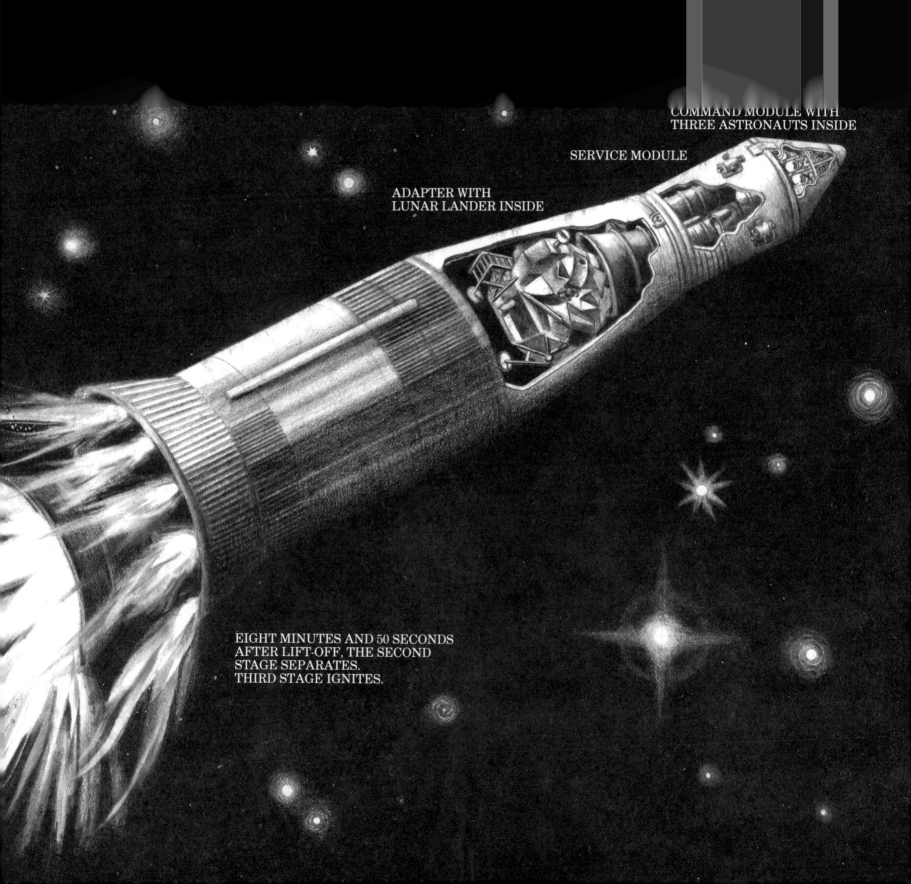

COMMAND MODULE WITH
THREE ASTRONAUTS INSIDE

SERVICE MODULE

ADAPTER WITH
LUNAR LANDER INSIDE

EIGHT MINUTES AND 50 SECONDS
AFTER LIFT-OFF, THE SECOND
STAGE SEPARATES.
THIRD STAGE IGNITES.

July 20, 1969
Sunday

We landed on the moon! I saw it on TV.

APOLLO 11

APOLLO 11 CREW: NEIL ARMSTRONG,
MICHAEL COLLINS, BUZZ ALDRIN

There is only one world in outer space people have ever visited. That is the moon, but no one walked on the moon until 1969.

The moon is very different from our world, the earth. On the moon, there is no air, no water, no clouds, no weather, and no sound. There are no plants or animals. The rolling, barren ground of the moon is covered with craters. There is nothing but gray rock and gray soil. The soil is like powder. It sticks to your boots.

Because there's no air to breathe on the moon, you must wear a space suit. That suit also keeps you from freezing at night and boiling during the day. Even the hottest and coldest places on earth are unable to match the moon. The daytime temperature on the moon is high enough to boil water (212 degrees above zero). At night, the temperature drops to about 280 degrees below zero.

On earth, air makes the sky look blue. Without air, the moon's sky always looks black. You never see a rosy sunrise, an orange sunset, or a purple twilight. Stars are out in the daytime. The only color you see is hanging in the sky. It's the blue earth.

The moon is a lot smaller than the earth. The earth is about 8,000 miles across and 25,000 miles around the middle. The moon is a little more than 2,000 miles across and about 6,800 miles around.

Gravity on the moon is much weaker. On the moon you weigh six times less than you weigh on earth. If you weigh sixty pounds on earth, you would weigh ten pounds on the moon.

Because you weigh less on the moon, you can jump six times higher there. A skateboard on the moon could hop a curb three feet high. If your house were on the moon, you could jump onto the roof.

In a baseball game on the moon, every hit would be a home run. You would reach first base in about ten steps. The game would never be called on account of rain. With no air to carry the sound, you could never hear the fans cheer at Moon Stadium.

People have been travel-
ing on the earth for more
than a hundred thousand
years. Why did it take so
long before anyone could
get to the moon? It's be-
cause the moon is far away
and hard to reach. The
moon is about 239,000 miles
(almost a quarter of a mil-
lion miles) from the earth.
You would have to line up
thirty earths in a row to
reach that distance.

MOON

239,000 MILES

(2,160 MILES ACROSS)

It's about 2,500 miles from one side of the United States to the other. If you could drive at 55 miles per hour without stopping, you would make the trip in a little less than two days. If you could drive to the moon at 55 miles per hour, it would take about six months to get there.

You need a rocket to travel from earth to the moon. It took the biggest rocket ever built to make that trip. The Apollo spacecraft landed on the moon on July 20, 1969, four days after it left earth. The first astronauts only stayed on the moon for six hours. They returned home to earth four days later.

EARTH

(7,926 MILES ACROSS)

Probably tens of thousands of years before we ever landed on the moon, people were looking at the moon and using it to count the days of the month. They were able to use the moon as a calendar because the moon seems to change shape every day. It is possible that Ice Age hunters in Europe kept track of the days by watching the moon change. Marks they made on pieces of bone may stand for each day's changing moon.

The changes in the shape of the moon are called the moon's phases, and there are three reasons why the moon seems to change.

First, the moon is round, like a ball.

Second, the moon shines like a mirror and gives off no light of its own. Sunlight bounces off of its surface.

Third, the moon travels around the earth.

If the moon were like a light bulb and glowed with its own light, it would look the same from every direction. You can walk around a lamp without a shade and see that the light bulb's shape doesn't change.

With a balloon and a flashlight you can see for yourself why the moon shines the way it does. First, draw a face on the balloon with a marker. Next, fasten the balloon to the end of a ruler so that the face is looking at you when you hold up the ruler. Ask someone to hold the flashlight at the far end of a dark room. When the flashlight is pointed toward you, it acts like the sun. You are like the earth, and the balloon is like the moon.

Start by holding the balloon out toward the flashlight with the face toward you. The balloon's face is completely dark, but as you turn slowly around, more and more of the face has light on it. By the time you turn half of the way toward the opposite direction, half of the face is shining. If the balloon were flat like a pizza, its shape wouldn't change this way. If you didn't move the balloon around you, it wouldn't change at all.

Light is always reflected from half of the balloon. How much light you see depends on where the balloon is and where the flashlight is. Keep turning until you are facing completely away from the flashlight. Now the face on the balloon is looking back toward the flashlight. The balloon's face is fully lit, and the other side—the side you can't see—is dark. If you keep turning, the light on the balloon's face will disappear. When it's all dark, the balloon and you will be back where it started.

ROBOT FOR HIRE
Cheap!
I clean rooms.

LEFT HALF LIT

WHAT YOU SEE

LIGHT

FACE ALL DARK

FACE ALL LIT

LIGHT

WHAT IT LOOKS LIKE
FROM THE CEILING

17

RIGHT HALF LIT

Sunlight is always falling on half of the moon and on half of the earth, too. We say it is daytime on the half of the earth that is in sunshine. On the dark half, we say it is night. Half of the moon is also in daylight, and half is in night.

When the moon is in the same direction as the sun, the dark half of the moon faces us here on the earth. We can't see any moon at all. We call this phase the new moon. If the moon never moved from this place, we would never see it.

The moon does move, however, and the path the moon follows around the earth is called its orbit. Each day it moves a little along that path. It is always round, like the balloon. Because it moves, each day we see a little more of the lighted moon.

At first, just a curved sliver of moon shows up. This shape is called a crescent (*kre-sent*). This moon is called a waxing crescent. Waxing is an old word that means "growing," and so we have a growing moon. Each time we see the moon, it looks a little bigger and a little brighter.

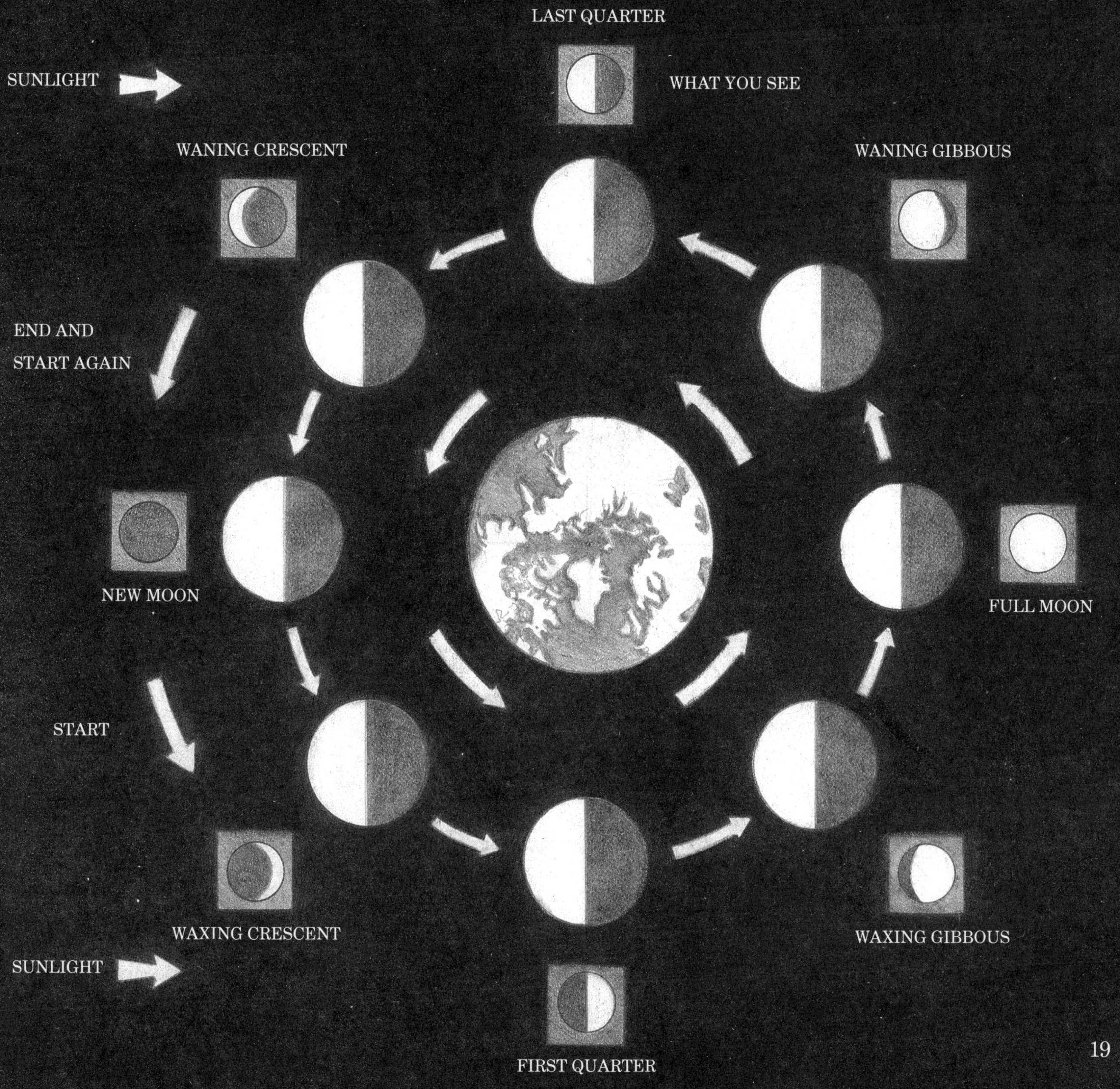

SUNLIGHT →

LAST QUARTER

WHAT YOU SEE

WANING CRESCENT

WANING GIBBOUS

END AND

START AGAIN

NEW MOON

FULL MOON

START

WAXING CRESCENT

WAXING GIBBOUS

SUNLIGHT →

FIRST QUARTER

19

NEW MOON **WAXING CRESCENT** **FIRST QUARTER** **WAXING GIBBOUS**

A week or so after new moon, half of the moon—the right half—is lit. Sometimes people call it a half moon. This phase is known, however, as first quarter. The moon is one-fourth of the way around its path and one-fourth of the way through its set of phases. When it goes all the way around, it will be back at the place for new moon.

A few more days go by, and the moon fills out more. Now it looks kind of oval. When the moon has this shape, it is called a gibbous (*gib-us*) moon.

Roughly two weeks after new moon, the moon reaches the side of its orbit farthest from the sun. Now the bright moon has the shape of a complete disk. This is the full moon, and you can read by its light. If the moon did not budge from this spot in its orbit, we would see a full moon every night.

FULL MOON   WANING GIBBOUS   LAST QUARTER   WANING CRESCENT

The Moon and You

Written by E.C. Krupp
Illustrated by Robin Rector Krupp

Macmillan

Krupp/Krupp   The Moon and You

21

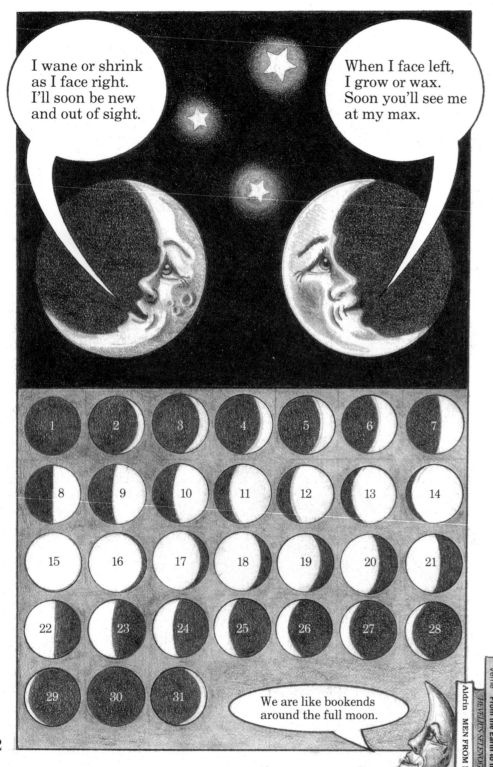

But the moon keeps moving. As it shifts back toward the sun, the sunlight is steadily shaved away. Now we say the moon is waning (*way-ning*). Waning is an old word that means "shrinking," and in this half of the cycle we have a shrinking moon.

At first the waning moon is a gibbous moon again, a little less round.

About a week after the full moon, there is only a half moon left. Now it is the left half that shines. This phase is called last quarter. It marks the beginning of the last fourth of the cycle.

By the time two or three more days go by, the moon looks like a crescent again. This is the waning crescent, and soon there will be no moon at all. By then, we shall be back to the new moon.

We can see how long it takes the moon to go through all of its phases by counting the days from one new moon to the next. It takes the moon twenty-nine and one-half days to go through the whole set.

If you look at a calendar, you see that almost every month is about this long. Most months have thirty or thirty-one days. People used to count the days of the month by watching the moon. That's why a calendar month lasts close to twenty-nine and one-half days.

THE EGYPTIAN GOD OSIRIS AND HIS SON
SEATED IN THE MOON'S DISK

Because each month the moon grows bright, then shrinks and disappears, and then appears again as a fresh new crescent, the ancient Egyptians said the moon was the god Osiris, who died and came back to life. The moon seems to come back to life every month.

23

The ancient Chinese also thought the moon could come back to life. They said that Heng O, the goddess of the moon, lives forever in the moon. A rabbit lives with her there and makes a potion that keeps her alive. The Chinese eat mooncakes in her honor each year at the Mid-Autumn Moon Festival.

DIAMOND RING

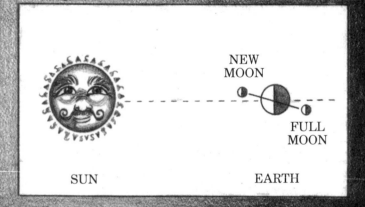

Most of the time the new moon isn't lined up exactly between the earth and sun. It may be a little above or a little below the place where the sun is. But sometimes the new moon crosses right in front of the sun. Then the moon almost perfectly blocks the sun. Really the sun is four hundred times bigger, but the sun is also four hundred times farther away. That makes the moon and the sun look exactly the same size. When the moon covers up the sun, the moon's shadow hits the earth, and we see an eclipse (*ee-klips*) of the sun.

DIAMOND RING

START HERE. IN AN ECLIPSE, THE MOON CROSSES OVER THE SUN FROM RIGHT TO LEFT.

TOTAL ECLIPSE

A partial eclipse makes it look as though something is taking a bite out of the sun. Many ancient people thought a dragon or other enemy was trying to eat the sun. In a total eclipse, the earth and sky get dark, and we get to see the glowing hot gas that surrounds the entire sun. This gas is called the corona (*kor-o-na*), which means "crown." The corona is always there, but it is too faint to see in the daytime.

KALA RAU, ECLIPSE MONSTER, ISLAND OF BALI

27

Sometimes the full moon lines up perfectly with the earth and the sun. When that happens, the moon passes through the earth's shadow. We see an eclipse of the moon. The eclipsed moon can turn a deep red. When this happened, the Vikings believed that one of the sky wolves had caught the full moon in its jaws and made it bleed.

I can't see the moon.

I'm between the sun and the moon.

I'm in the earth's shadow.

SUN

EARTH

MOON

Legends say the full moon can turn certain people into werewolves. Some people believe the full moon has the power to make people act strangely. Hospitals are supposed to have more emergencies at full moon, and there are supposed to be more crimes then, too. None of this is true.

HIGH TIDE

LOW TIDE

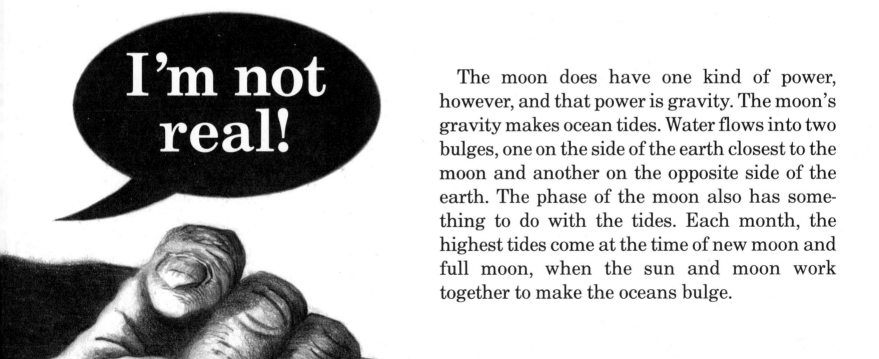

I'm not real!

The moon does have one kind of power, however, and that power is gravity. The moon's gravity makes ocean tides. Water flows into two bulges, one on the side of the earth closest to the moon and another on the opposite side of the earth. The phase of the moon also has something to do with the tides. Each month, the highest tides come at the time of new moon and full moon, when the sun and moon work together to make the oceans bulge.

MAN AND WOMAN TEWA HARVEST DANCERS,
SANTA CLARA PUEBLO, NEW MEXICO

When you say the word month, you're really using a word which used to mean "moon." People all over the world once named each moon after what was happening in that month's time of the year. The Tewa Indians of New Mexico called one of the cold winter months the "ice moon." "The month when leaves break out" happened in spring, when leaves started to appear on trees. Two months later, it was the moon for "corn planting."

In the fall, the
"moon of falling leaves"
marked the changing seasons
for the Tewa. Because it was time
to gather the corn, other Indians named
it the "harvest month." Have you heard of the
harvest moon? That's what we call the moon in September
around the time it is full. That bright moon provides extra light
after sundown and helps farmers work late to bring in the grain. 33

Hindu

Maya

Roman

My **Moon Collection**
Can you find all 15 moons?

Moslem

At least five thousand years ago, the ancient Egyptians made a calendar out of the moon's changes. Others, including the Babylonians, the Chinese, the Hindus of India, the Greeks, and the Romans also based their calendar on the moon. The ancient Maya of Mexico and Central America counted the days of the moon. So did the Incas of Peru. The Jewish calendar and the Muslim calendar still use the moon to start and end the month.

Egyptian

DEZIEMBRE
CAPACINTIDAIMI

Inca

Hebrew

Babylonian

Chinese

1969   **JULY**   **1969**

SUN	MON	TUES	WED	THURS	FRI	SAT
		1	2	3	4	5
6	7	8	9	10	11	12
13	14	15	16	17	18	
20	21	22	23	24	25	26
27	28	29	30	31		

LAST QUARTER

NEW MOON

Apollo II lifts off for the moon!

We walk on the moon

!!! FIRST QUARTER

Splash down in Pacific Ocean!

FULL MOON

You can watch the moon yourself and see that its phases don't start and stop with the months in the calendar we use. The full moon doesn't just come at the middle of the month. It can come at any time.

♪ ♫ BLUE MOON ♫♪

MARCH 1999

SUN	MON	TUES	WED	THURS	FRI	SAT
	1	2 ○	3	4	5	6
7	8	9 ◐	10	11	12	13
14	15	16 ●	17	18	19	20
21	22	23 ◑	24	25	26	27
28	29	30	31 ○			

Last blue moon of the century

Sometimes—but not very often—we get two full moons in one month. That second full moon is called a "blue moon." No one knows why. Now we say "once in a blue moon" to mean "once in a long time."

The moon doesn't really look blue. Most of the time its color is white. What color does it look to you? Maybe it looks silver. You can tell, however, especially when the moon is full, that the moon's color is not even. Some parts are darker. Some people think they can see a face or an animal or an entire person in the light and dark areas on the moon. What do you see?

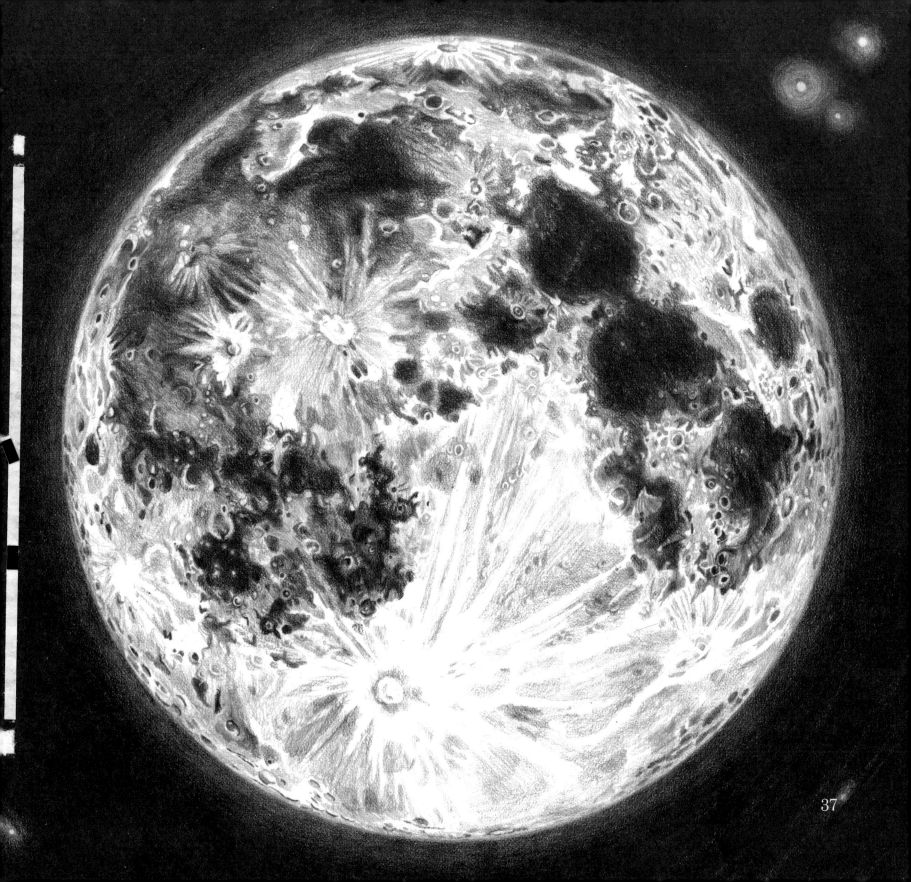

37

Some people say the face they see in the moon is the Man in the Moon, but not everyone sees a man in the moon. The Maori people of New Zealand see a woman in the moon. Her name is Rona.

The Haida Indians, who live on islands close to British Columbia, in Canada, say the woman in the moon carries a bucket.

Some of the people of Siberia and Lapland also believe there is a girl in the moon.

In ancient Greece, the moon was the goddess Selene, who rode through the sky in a silver chariot.

According to the Vikings, the dark shapes on the moon are really a boy and girl who went to get a pail of water and were kidnapped to the moon. This pair is really Jack and Jill. You know about them from the nursery rhyme.

MAYA

AZTEC

ANOTHER WAY TO SEE THE RABBIT

ONE WAY TO SEE THE RABBIT

Quite a few people thought there is a rabbit in the moon. The dark spots do look more like a rabbit than a man in the moon. The ancient Aztec of Mexico, the Maya, the prehistoric Mimbres Indians of the Southwest, the people of India, southeast Asia, and Korea, and the Japanese all could see a rabbit in the moon.

MIMBRES

JAPANESE

CHINESE

LOOK AT THE WHITE SHAPE
TO SEE THE TOAD

Remember the rabbit the Chinese said lived on the moon with Heng O the moon goddess? That's the same rabbit. The Chinese also said that Heng O was turned into a toad and that you can see the toad in the moon, too.

41

I'm always looking at you, kid!

Whatever picture you may see in the moon, it is always the same. The Man in the Moon is always looking at us. That's because the same side of the moon always faces the earth. The other side always faces away from us. Why is that?

As the moon moves around the earth, it also turns a little each day. That's how it keeps the same side toward the earth. The earth's gravity keeps the moon in its orbit, and the earth's gravity has also made the moon turn at just the right speed to keep one side facing the earth. It took billions of years for the earth's gravity to lock one side of the moon in our direction. If the moon didn't turn this way, we would see different sides of it when it travels around the earth. So the moon is spinning, but it spins slowly. The earth spins around once every twenty-four hours and gives us day and night. The moon spins around once in a little less than a month. This means daytime on the moon lasts about two weeks, and so does night.

MOON ORBITS
WITH SLOW SPIN

MOON ORBITS
WITH NO SPIN

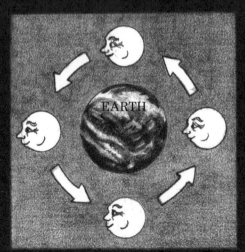

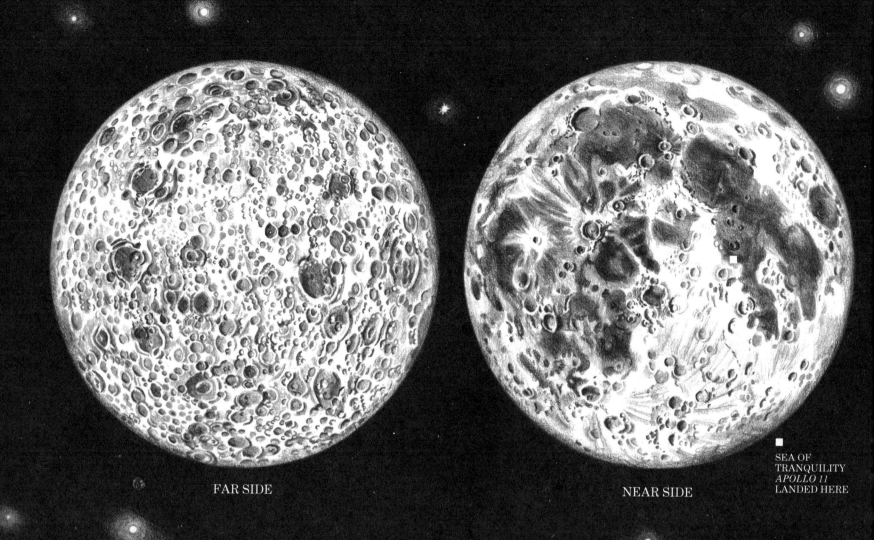

FAR SIDE

NEAR SIDE

SEA OF
TRANQUILITY
APOLLO 11
LANDED HERE

The other side of the moon is the far side. It's daylight there when our side of
the moon is dark, at new moon. The far side is all dark when our side is full.
    No one knew what the far side of the moon looked like until 1959 when the
Russians sent the *Luna 3* space probe around the back to take the first
photographs of it. It does not have as many dark areas as you can see on the
near side. We think that means the crust on the far side is thicker.

The bright and dark areas on the moon are really different kinds of land. The bright places are highlands. They are mostly hills and mountains. A telescope shows us many round pits there, too. These pits are craters. We find them all over the moon, and almost every one of them was made by a meteorite that crashed into the moon. A meteorite (*mee-tee-oh-rite*) is just a rock from space. When one hits, the explosion hollows out a crater.

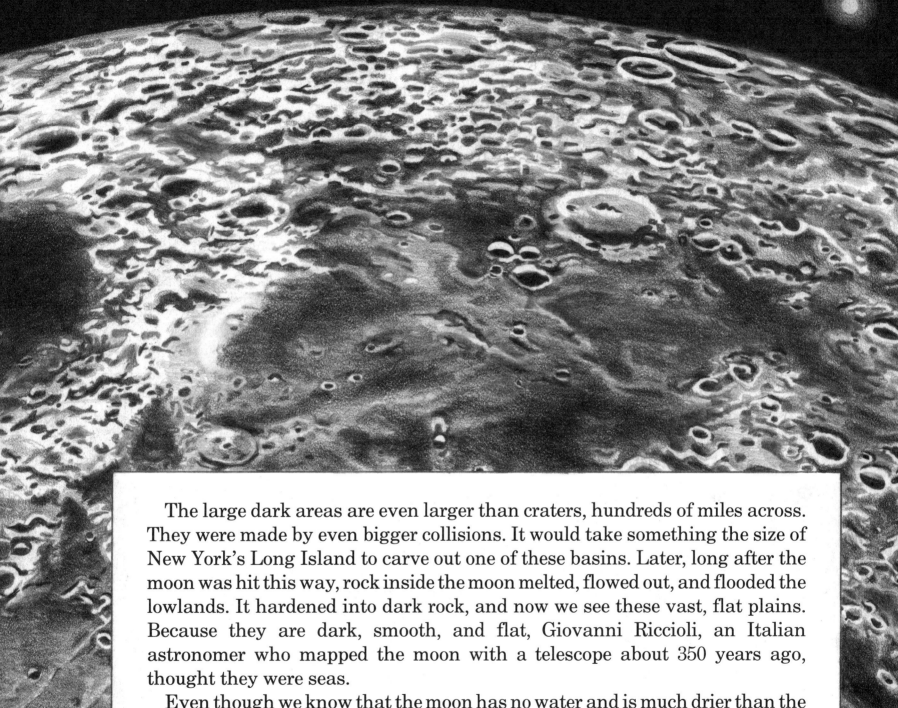

The large dark areas are even larger than craters, hundreds of miles across. They were made by even bigger collisions. It would take something the size of New York's Long Island to carve out one of these basins. Later, long after the moon was hit this way, rock inside the moon melted, flowed out, and flooded the lowlands. It hardened into dark rock, and now we see these vast, flat plains. Because they are dark, smooth, and flat, Giovanni Riccioli, an Italian astronomer who mapped the moon with a telescope about 350 years ago, thought they were seas.

Even though we know that the moon has no water and is much drier than the driest desert on earth, we still call them "seas." The first people from earth to set foot on the moon landed on the Sea of Tranquility.

Some of the moon rocks brought back to earth by the Apollo astronauts turned out to be the oldest rocks we know. They tell us the moon was formed about four and one-half billion (4,500,000,000) years ago. The astronauts also did experiments to learn about the inside of the moon. Unlike the earth, the moon is probably all rock. The earth's core is melted metal.

HARDENED LAVA AND OTHER TYPES OF ROCKS WERE COLLECTED BY ASTRONAUTS.

SCIENTIST-ASTRONAUT DR. HARRISON H. SCHMITT AND HUGE MOON BOULDER ON THE LAST APOLLO MISSION

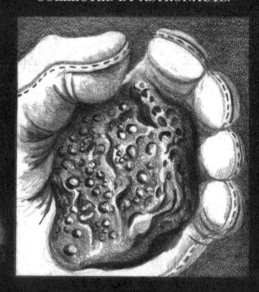

Some scientists think the moon formed in a crash between the earth and another, smaller world. They were like a pair of cosmic bumper cars. The earth swallowed up the heavy core of the other world. The lighter outer part of that world was left in orbit around the earth. Gravity soon pulled it together into the moon we now have.

We don't know for sure exactly how the moon first formed. We need to study the moon some more. The last time anyone went to the moon was 1972. Only

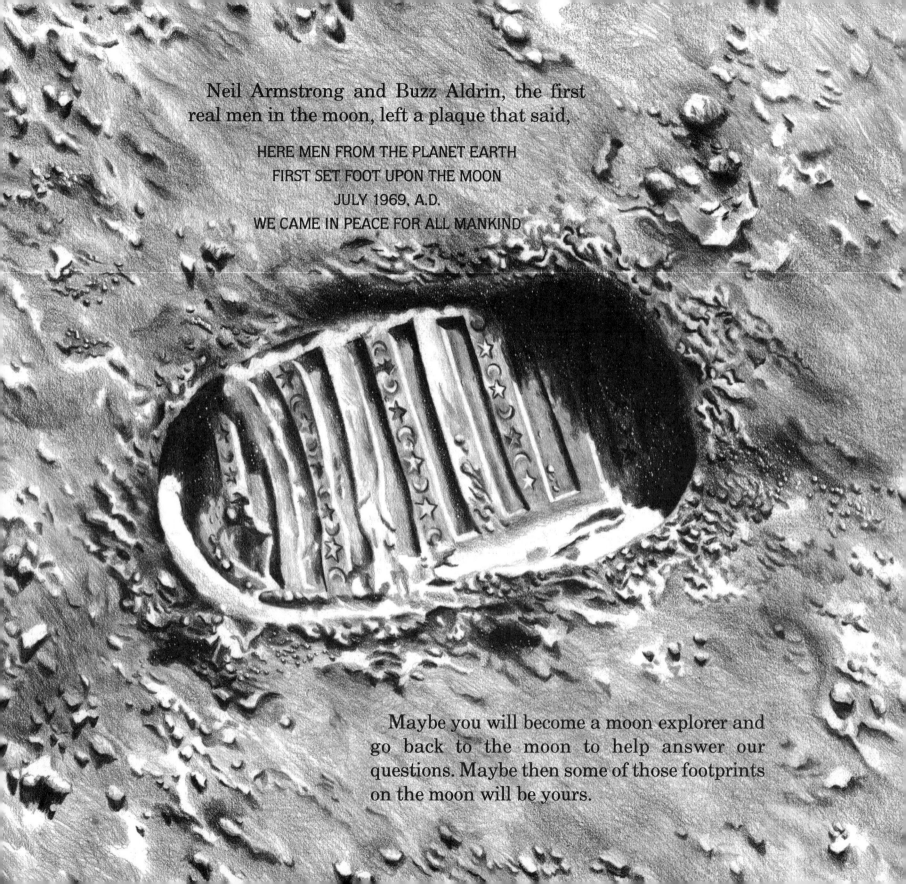

Neil Armstrong and Buzz Aldrin, the first
real men in the moon, left a plaque that said,

HERE MEN FROM THE PLANET EARTH
FIRST SET FOOT UPON THE MOON
JULY 1969, A.D.
WE CAME IN PEACE FOR ALL MANKIND

Maybe you will become a moon explorer and
go back to the moon to help answer our
questions. Maybe then some of those footprints
on the moon will be yours.